Paper-Whites for
Lady Jane

Poems of a Midlife Love Affair

Books by LOUIS DANIEL BRODSKY

Poetry

Five Facets of Myself   (1967)* (1995)
The Easy Philosopher   (1967)* (1995)
"A Hard Coming of It" and Other Poems   (1967)* (1995)
The Foul Rag-and-Bone Shop   (1967)* (1969)* (1995)
Points in Time   (1971)* (1995)
Taking the Back Road Home   (1972)*
Trip to Tipton and Other Compulsions   (1972)*
"The Talking Machine" and Other Poems   (1973)*
Cold, Companionable Streams   (1974)*
Tiffany Shade   (1974)*
Trilogy: A Birth Cycle   (1974)
Monday's Child   (1975)
Preparing for Incarnations   (1975) (1976)
The Kingdom of Gewgaw   (1976)
Point of Americas II   (1976)
La Preciosa   (1977)
Stranded in the Land of Transients   (1978)
The Uncelebrated Ceremony of Pants Factory Fatso   (1978)
Birds in Passage   (1980)
Résumé of a Scrapegoat   (1980)
Mississippi Vistas: Volume One of *A Mississippi Trilogy*   (1983) (1990)
You Can't Go Back, Exactly   (1988)
The Thorough Earth   (1989)
Four and Twenty Blackbirds Soaring   (1989)
Falling from Heaven: Holocaust Poems of a Jew and a Gentile
    (with William Heyen)   (1991)
Forever, for Now: Poems for a Later Love   (1991)
Mistress Mississippi: Volume Three of *A Mississippi Trilogy*   (1992)
A Gleam in the Eye: Poems for a First Baby   (1992)
Gestapo Crows: Holocaust Poems   (1992)
The Capital Café: Poems of Redneck, U.S.A.   (1993)
Disappearing in Mississippi Latitudes: Volume Two of *A Mississippi
    Trilogy*   (1994)
A Mississippi Trilogy: A Poetic Saga of the South   (1995)*
Paper-Whites for Lady Jane: Poems of a Midlife Love Affair   (1995)

Bibliography (Coedited with Robert Hamblin)

Selections from the William Faulkner Collection of Louis Daniel Brodsky:
  A Descriptive Catalogue   (1979)
Faulkner: A Comprehensive Guide to the Brodsky Collection
    Volume I: The Bibliography   (1982)
    Volume II: The Letters   (1984)
    Volume III: *The De Gaulle Story*   (1984)
    Volume IV: *Battle Cry*   (1985)
    Volume V: Manuscripts and Documents   (1989)
Country Lawyer and Other Stories for the Screen by William Faulkner   (1987)
Stallion Road: A Screenplay by William Faulkner   (1989)

Biography

William Faulkner, Life Glimpses   (1990)

Novels

The Adventures of the Night Riders, Better Known as the Terrible Trio
  (with Richard Milsten)   (1960)*
Between Grief and Nothing   (1964)*
Between the Heron and the Wren   (1965)*
Dink Phlager's Alligator   *(novella)*   (1966)*
The Drift of Things   (1966)*
Vineyard's Toys   (1967)*
The Bindlestiffs   (1968)*

* *Unpublished*

Paper-Whites for Lady Jane

Poems of a Midlife Love Affair

by

Louis Daniel Brodsky

Louis Daniel Brodsky

12/30/07

St. Louis, MO

TIME BEING BOOK**S**
POETRY IN SIGHT AND SOUND
St. Louis, Missouri

Time Being Books®
10411 Clayton Road
St. Louis, Missouri 63131

Time Being Books® is an imprint of Time Being Press®
St. Louis, Missouri

Time Being Press® is a 501(c)(3) not-for-profit organization.

Time Being Books® volumes are printed on acid-free paper, and binding materials are chosen for strength and durability.

ISBN 1-877770-95-7 (Hardcover)
ISBN 1-877770-96-5 (Paperback)

Library of Congress Cataloging-in-Publication Data:

Brodsky, Louis Daniel.
    Paper-whites for Lady Jane : poems of a mid-life love affair / by
    Louis Daniel Brodsky.
        p.   cm.
      ISBN 1-877770-95-7 (cloth). — ISBN 1-877770-96-5 (pbk.)
      1. Love poetry, American.   I. Title.
    PS3552.R623P3   1995
    811'.54 — dc20
                                                            95-42905
                                                            CIP

Cover art by Michael Eisemann, *La Musique*. Permission granted
    by El-Baz Gallery, New York, N.Y.
Book design and typesetting by Lori Loesche and Cynthia Higgins
Manufactured in the United States of America

First Edition, first printing (December 1995)

Acknowledgments

I would like to express my thanks to Jerry Call, Editor in Chief, Sheri Vandermolen, Editor, and Cynthia Higgins, Assistant Editor, of Time Being Books for their close, sensitive reading of the manuscript and for their many suggestions, which have considerably refined the poems in this book.

I also wish to make grateful acknowledgment to the editors of these publications, in which the following poems, in earlier versions, originally appeared: *Painted Bride Quarterly* ("November Planting"); *Portland Review* ("Statues"); *Route One* ("A Part of History"); and the *St. Louis Jewish Light* ("Breathing Eye to Eye," "Gaining a Better Perspective," "Making Sweet Music," "Nightflowers," "November Planting," "A Valentine for Lady Jane").

Janie,

I give you these pages,

my paper-whites,

in return for all the lovely flowers

you've grown in my heart's garden

these past six years.

Narcissus

Another short-trumpet species is the *poet's narcissus*. It produces a single, wide-open blossom on each stalk. Generally, the blossom has white petals surrounding a short, yellowish cup with a crinkled red edge.

The *paperwhite narcissus* is a short-trumpet species that can be grown indoors in winter from bulbs placed on pebbles. Most cultivated types have large clusters of pure white flowers that are very heavily scented. When breeders cross the paperwhite narcissus with the poet's narcissus, they get improved varieties, including types with flowers of two different colors on the same plant. People value these beautiful hybrids.

— The World Book Encyclopedia

Contents

Paper-Whites for Lady Jane

Poems of a Midlife Love Affair

* This symbol is used to indicate that a stanza has been divided because of pagination.

November Planting

Less than three weeks ago, sweet Jane,
You chose a spacious crystal bowl
In which to place your baker's dozen of paper-white bulbs
And set them free to do their majestical growing.
Periodically, while relaxing in the living room,
We've marked their progress:
Thick, vermiculate roots spreading like creepers,
Larger than life for watery refraction,
Their slender stems thrusting upward
Like cylindrical skyscrapers —
The entire fibrous network God's architecture.

This Sunday morning, we luxuriate in sleep,
Uneager to leave dreams Vaughan Williams seeded
With his *Fantasia on a Theme by Thomas Tallis*
As a prelude to our own musical blooming:
Sending down roots, blending, tendrils sprouting.
Eventually we awaken into November's silent greenhouse,
Brew coffee, then linger by the narcissus cluster,
Erotic with white-petaled nebulae,
Whose pungence is the same scent
We remember inundating us last night
As we entered the earth together.

11/26/90

Greenhouse Effects

Something there is profoundly anomalous
That confounds my senses
Once the mind has decreed them winterbound,
Then finds them spending outdoors
The entire 76-degree afternoon.
I stroll hand in hand with Lady Jane,
Pausing in the sun
To watch the prodigiously social prairie dogs
Dig additional tunnels
Connecting their utterly public
Private underground towns.
We vicariously applaud with overeager seals
And sea lions being fed fresh fish
In their nearby ocean
By the trainer/keeper/maintenance man —
Oh, how we admire their smooth, sleek sensuality!
We postpone our tour just long enough
To witness, within arm's reach,
Two colossally vain, Seuss-like peacocks preening,
Oblivious of danger from humans like us.

Lady Jane squeezes my hand,
Confirms her juices are flowing,
Rushing, flooding freely
As though she were coursing through my bloodstream
Toward the source of my pulsing libido.
It seems strange, if predictably so,
How always on a sunny spring or fall day at the zoo
Our hormones run crazy,
Exciting in us the wondrous plundering of pure animality,
Inciting our fantasies to riot, change skin,
Climb inside cages or behind bouldered confines,
And reappear in tiger or zebra stripes
Or the two-tone hide of a Malayan tapir,
Better yet, revel in the gaiety of the polar bear
Diving continually into its pool
To cool itself against November's inordinate heat
*

And cavorting with a beachball
It can't quite balance
On the tip of its perfectly white delight —
Like we're doing right this minute.

11/27/90

A White Christmas

I awaken tentatively into this still morning;
I'm the only creature stirring.
My lady and her son resist resurrection,
Let sleep bathe them in sweet dreams.
I shower, then roam from one end of the house
To the other remote end
Before wandering toward a picture window.

At this hour, I witness a very orange sun
Trying to pry apart glistening pines
Buffering the eastern extremities of this property
To reach gigantic icicles fastened to the eaves
Of this pagodalike pavilion,
Sheltering me from piercing, sub-zero reality
This pristine Christmas morn.

I know it will be days, maybe weeks,
Before vision from this vantage
Will relinquish its stalactitic configuration,
Months until the trees will commence their greening,
And years, if ever, before this holiday,
Inflated with decades of faded familial memories,
Will disintegrate into forgetting and let me start fresh.

Nonetheless, I recognize my need today
To get as far away from depression
As circumstances will permit.
I brew coffee, take a seat by the fireplace,
Focus on the three stockings bulging with treats,
And attempt to repress every extraneous echo
That might reconnect me with my past.

After all, I'm the self-proclaimed "new man,"
He who's survived divorce
And, at 49, arrived emaciated of spirit
To be taken in as a refugee and repatriated
By the lady of this magnificent St. Louis residence,
My beloved Jane,
Who, like me, defies description,

Refuses to be stereotyped,
Prefers instead to live outside society,
Behind the privacy her vast estate provides.
Despite my empty pockets and blasted hopes,
Providence has brought me here.
Quietly, gratefully, I pray to Elohim,
Trusting He has mandated this fate for me,

And sigh a promise to reject complacency
Whenever it threatens my mission
To translate His faith in mankind to the world
Through my fragile yet durable verse.
Moreover, I proclaim my faith in humanity
By whispering sympathy to my apostate ex-wife
And love-wishes to my distant children this yuletide day.

As I sit sipping silence from this mystical cup,
My lips begin to quiver;
Its draught must belong to a mythical rite
That has somehow discovered me just in time.
When I look up, Janie kisses me;
Petals of paper-white fragrance
Fill my eyes with her Christmas snow.

12/25/90

Scents of Wonderment

The sky below which I drive home tonight
Is twilight's epiphany:
A crisscross of orange and violet hues
Suspending day's blue jardiniere,
In which nightfall's flowers already are blossoming.
Soon I'll inspire their perfume
And saturate my imagination
With pungent fragrance reminiscent of paper-whites
My lady forced from tumescent bulbs
She half submerged in crystal bowls about our house
To whet my sex-buds, coax them into opening.

Coursing north, I witness a metamorphosis:
Dusk's stratocumulus blooms close,
Leaving no traces of that illusional bouquet
Except those I know never existed anyway
In their colossal sky-bowl,
Those I also know will continue growing
No matter where I go
Since (as it was in the Beginning
And shall be in the End) every invention,
Whether God's or man's, is of the same intention:
To perpetuate a "scents of wonderment."

12/26/90

Exploring New Worlds

So distant from my family land
And my sadly misguided wife of two decades,
Who precipitated my heart's anarchy
And its unplanned banishment
From my marriage, my children, my home,
I contemplate, this entire New Year's Day,
The treacherous journey I took getting here,
The immigration I've made to the peaceful reaches
Of a more hospitable world,
And, in an ironic sense,
Celebrate my unanticipated independence.

I spend this quiet holiday afternoon
Reading essays by the country's leading historians
About the settlers of our New England coast,
Its initially hostile clime,
Their travail with America's aborigines,
And how the Protestants, those heroic souls
Of Jamestown, Plymouth, the Massachusetts Bay Colony,
Adapted by taming the wilderness
To augment their freedom
From religious persecution and regal tyranny,
And I'm amazed by the coincidence of our differences.

This day, I give thanks for safe passage,
Secure roof, food that nourishes me daily
And pray that the covenant just entered into
Between myself and this second new year
Of the 20th century's last decade
Will manifest a healthy and successful destiny for me,
My lady, and our extended families.
May divine Providence enlighten our commonwealth
With God's creativity and mighty love
And, on our next exploration,
Let Janie and me discover Eden's eastern shores.

1/1/91

Breathing Eye to Eye

After the newness has passed,
The adhesive that keeps passion intact,
Makes the original sense of wonderment last,
Is the desire for giving up old habits
Lovers might have initially disguised
Or deceived themselves into believing they'd jettisoned
As sacrifices to an incipient relationship
And for recommitting the heart's allegiance
To another human life,

Just as we've done, my affectionate lady,
Watching candles you lit,
Their tips flickering the fragrances of our lovemaking,
Change mystically into paper-whites
Illuminating the bedroom with our blooms.
Transfigurations such as this
Come once a lifetime, night after night,
To those who, seeing beyond their noses,
Breathe through their eyes.

1/3/91

Listening to the Waves

Sitting on this tiny balcony facing the ocean,
Ten stories high,
Janie and I gaze down at the hotel patio,
Vertiginous as Alice
Peering at a nervous white rabbit
Escaping into a bottomless hole
Leading to the queen's manicured gardens;
Its convoluted tile paths
Maze through profuse plantings
Of sea grapes, palms, exotic flowers.
Our eyes pan north and south,
Along tan, sandy beaches
Perforated by cabanas, umbrellas,
And people worshiping prostrate to the sun god.

We share this Saturday morning's solitude,
Listening, just listening, to the waves
Tripping over themselves
Moving forward, heading shoreward,
Some breaking prematurely
As if reaching orgasm without being coaxed,
Others eluding explosion,
Seeming to flow back out unbroken,
Leaving behind in their inconspicuous receding
A thieves' market of debris
But otherwise no traces of their destinations
Or places of origin;
We've always wished to believe
Intent listening engenders wisdom.

Occasional noise shakes our concentration:
Helicopters jackhammering the air,
Single-engine planes laboring in cross winds,
Jetliners taking off uproariously
Beyond Port Everglades,
And water turkeys squawking,
Awkwardly plunging or reeling out to sea.
But the ocean's voice remains dominant,
A timeless, fluid oracle,
*

Whose prophecies mesmerize us
With their inscrutable lucidity.
We listen to the waves' unpredictable litany
As if this time
They might invite us home.

1/26/91

Ports of Call

Last week, my fair lady and I
Retreated to Fort Lauderdale for six days
And stayed at a hotel on the beach,
A thousand yards north of Port Everglades,
In a balconied tenth-floor room,
From which we watched the ocean at play
Beneath winter's 80-degree rays.

Oh, the images from that vantage that persist:
Skies filled with rambunctious vapors,
Water turkeys and sea gulls,
Parasails, and radial-engine airplanes
Trailing banners advertising the "good life,"
Tankers anchored a mile offshore,
Waiting to make berth in a busy harbor,

Sunbathers, swimmers, shellers,
Beachcombers strolling alone or hand in hand.
Those and so many more strands
Did we weave into the magic carpet we rode
Over dreaming's Terra Nova
On our trip south out of time,
When we sipped of the Fountain's elixir,

That we almost can't reconcile ourselves
To this frigid St. Louis blast,
Almost can't convince our vexed intellects
To correct sea-level settings
And accept our present location
As just another port of call
Along the landfall we're planning to explore.

1/30/91

Lovers' Sunday

Now, the four o'clock Lord's-day sun,
So glorious in its warmth,
Suffuses our flesh with pleasurable lassitude.
Together, Jane and I have measured the afternoon
From its origin at the Sunshine Inn,
Where we savored brunch —
She, the fresh-fruit plate and date-nut bread,
I, blueberry-and-granola pancakes
And Viennese coffee — to gentle lovemaking
Under the influence of David Benoit,
Whose rapturously struck jazz piano keys,
Loaded to passion's threshold,
Sent us to that invisible star
Where we keep our most intimate hearts.

And, oh, what we discovered there,
Where marrow and bone echo our heritage,
Arteries and veins irrigate ancestral lands
Long ago forgotten by us
Despite demands we force on ourselves,
And brains generate oracles,
Whose promises kiss our lips with hope,
Guide our innocent spirits
Into such unself-conscious coital positions
We might as easily be newborn fawns,
Nestled securely beneath the great mothering shadow,
Covered with placental juices,
Safe in our wet nakedness,
As souls in love since time's first Sunday.

2/10/91

A Valentine for Lady Jane

Driving home to you
This tempestuous afternoon
From a location two days away,
Aimlessly watching stolid cows,
Huddled against penetrating winds,
And ramshackle farmhouses and barns
Leaning like Cape Cod weather vanes
In the same direction the gale force blows,
I drift into my own time zone,
Defined solely by the outline of your face,
And occupy the idle miles ahead
China-painting your delicate features with my mind.

Edging northerly, ever closer to St. Louis,
Through sporadic pockets of snow,
I grow increasingly less self-reliant,
More dependent upon the silences we engender
Whenever we share love's language
And on the Adam and Eve laughter we spark
Engaging each other's quick, oft sardonic wit
And treasure chest of fresh, zesty, fractured aphorisms.
As I return through white-stippled sunshine,
Unmissing you is my one ambition.
Until I'm with you again,
We'll be equal parts of the same broken heart.

2/14/91

Planting by Dream-Light

Last evening, sweet Saturday eve,
You and I, Janie,
Seeded each other's dreams with passion
So ecstatically,
Miraculously bright
Its blooms illumined the black sky,
Kept me up all night.

This morning, you told me
Your blood had circulated so fast,
So ecstatically,
That you couldn't sleep either,
Also stayed awake,
Seeding our dark garden
With today's bright blooms.

3/10/91

Time in a Bottle

Oh, if only last evening at the symphony
Were a bottle filled with magic soap,
Into whose dazzling, faceted glass body
I could dip imagination's wand,
Coat it with bubble-notes,
Lift it to my lips, and, like an oboist,
Blow whisperously into the moment,
Then I could recreate you and me
By catching in my palm
Each floating, iridescent sphere,
Savoring its evanescent wetness
As though it were a falling snowflake
Or a tear collecting in your eye
For my fingertip to wipe dry —
Tiny, sibilant shimmer-shapes of happiness
You and I celebrated at Powell Hall,
Listening to the orchestra majestically perform
Ives' *Three Places in New England*,
Mahler's Symphony no. 1
And, in Sibelius' Violin Concerto in D Minor,
Accompany the stunning virtuosity
Of nineteen-year-old Midori,
Bowing impossibly intricate solo passages
On a Guarnerius del Gesù
That might have been made from the bones of a saint,
Not the mere wood of a tree felled near the Alps.

Oh, if only time were submissive
And could surrender to manipulation
By poets, musicians, magicians, and *amateurs*
Hoping to discourage forgetfulness
From denying them the pleasures of recollection,
Memory would be as accessible as you are
Right this minute, my beautiful, naked lady,
Rousing drowsily from dreams,
Nestling into my waiting body, breasts to chest,
Thighs tightening around me,
Inviting me to collaborate
*

In composing our own romantic concerto.
Ah, but then, who would care about the past
If they knew how to keep reinventing the future,
As we do, Janie, one day at a time?

3/17/91

Inland Sea

Although we sense Easter and Passover
Coming soon into full bloom,
Unfolding like jonquils, crocuses, and star magnolias,
We know nothing can keep us tied down,
Homebound in our secular temple
This shirt-sleeve Palm Sunday afternoon.
The open road, what little's left of it,
Compels us to drive away
With only the clothes on our backs,
Not even enough cash,
If plastic wampum fails, to barter for lunch.

Traveling light, we float above the highway,
Out of the city, up 270 to 67,
Approaching both bridged rivers,
First the Missouri, then the Mississippi,
Overflowing saturated shores, licking piers,
With diamond-flecked surfaces
Flaunting their cumulative thrust.
Coursing against such atavistic force,
We resist their demands on the land
By meandering to Alton,
Then westerly along barge-dotted Old Man to Grafton.

What a commanding view possesses us:
Massive, stratified limestone cliffs to our right,
Huck's and Jim's gateway to freedom
Coercing us from the port side.
Somehow, our shorebound sports car
Becomes a raft or flatboat or pirogue
We two tiny beings have cast adrift
At the gratuitous mercy of this Father of Waters,
Which we must trust won't condemn us today,
In the way its oceanic brother did Ishmael,
To dive into a white whale's Heidelberg tun

And survive to describe to future readers,
Stranded, huddled, frightened in the land's lee,
What it's like to be set loose for a lifetime
With no responsibilities except to persevere,
To believe in whatever undefined divine design
*

Might be operating at any given time.
This afternoon, driving parallel to the river,
We feel its draining current
Persuading, urging us east
Even as we press stubbornly upstream
Past Piasa toward Père Marquette State Park.

But before we reach our destination,
We arrive in Grafton and, heeding the call,
Explore its "quaint" craft and "antique" shops,
Stroll for a while with crowds from the city,
Come to browse, bargain hunt,
Let the lazy Sunday hours entertain them
With play only children luxuriate in daily.
But our eyes weary of collectibles and reproductions,
Lame paintings, silk flowers, quilts,
Imported bric-a-brac glutting tables, sills, ceilings,
Every inch of these renovated shacks.

At a snack-shop gas station on the main street,
The only solvent business in town,
We try to revive ourselves with coffee and doughnuts,
Then, deciding to quit for the day,
Buckle into our seats again for the return journey.
At once, we register a conspicuously missing essence:
Call it magic, name it mystification,
Whatever humans do
To prime their minds for new experiences.
We discuss the bluffs, blossoming flowers,
Almost to the exclusion of the water to our right,

And seem to forget even why we've made this trek.
Soon, Alton, its Victorian roofs and pinnacles
Jigsawing the horizon, its rickety bridge,
And its ubiquitous grain elevators all ashimmer,
Overtakes our vision; we grow anxious,
Remain so for the next forty-five minutes
As St. Louis chews us into pieces
Small enough to swallow; then we're home,
More exhausted than we thought possible,
But home safe, maybe like twin Ishmaels
Capable of relating our tale

On the outside chance that anyone,
Tomorrow or next week or ever,
Might wish to know how it felt to ignore,
For a precious hiatus, all necessities
And yield to whatever notions might materialize
Just for the sake of availing oneself
To any weight that trips the brain's lever,
Actuates imagination's mainspring.
And if we find nobody willing to listen,
We'll at least keep alive
That instinct to head upstream periodically.

3/25/91

Statues

I awaken into a sunny, 59th Street morning —
New York is bracing this April,
Exhilarating!
My blood rushes and gushes
Through perfectly synchronized auricles and ventricles
Like water recirculating in pipes
Of The Plaza's Aphrodite fountain,
Gravitating toward its pumping source
To be forced into soaring orgasm again.

I would ravish, in broad daylight,
The lady whose towel is forever suspended,
Poised to drape her naked, dripping torso,
Were it not for so many sightseers
Observing her tasteful striptease.
I linger long enough to memorize her posture;
As I gaze at her breasts, callipygian buttocks,
And softly rounded belly,
I feel my whole body turn hot.

I watch her cast-bronze figure grow fluid,
Dissolve slowly into the pool below,
Until nothing is left atop the pedestal
Where my eyes first encountered her aphrodisiacal shape
Except the shimmering image of you, Janie,
Stepping from the shower, dropping your bath towel,
Slipping, still wet,
Into bed with me last night,
The two of us flowing through love's cascade.

4/4/91

Flea-Marketing

For two days now, in New York City,
Possibly due to the inordinately early April warmth,
All street scenes have dovetailed
Like joints in Victorian furniture
Cluttering the dark corners of my imagination's attic.

What exactly I'm seeking up here,
Pulling out, rummaging through,
Shutting so many compartments and drawers,
Opening others, may be one or a hundred surprises
Hiding under accumulating disillusionments

Or, more likely, if not an overlooked insight
From previous trips to the edge of vision,
A new view, uniquely suited to me and you,
Sweet lady, who've accompanied me
To this flea market in the garden district

In quest of something others name
For its appearance or function and call a bargain
When they've alchemized a sow's ear into a silk purse
They fill with an entire afternoon's energy,
Fool's gold they'll schlep home,

Muse over for a few hours or weeks
Before quietly disposing of it in a convenient closet
Or dresser stored in the basement.
This Lord's morning,
While you still sleep, recuperating from fatigue

Both of us have experienced in our intense search
For two things that can't be quantified,
Adventure and love,
I contemplate today's activities
And fantasize SoHo becoming Cíbola or Atlantis.

Soon you'll join me forty stories below,
Where, together,
We'll set out to collect every image
Our eyes might transform to adorn a Crystal Palace
We'll inhabit for the rest of our visionary days.

4/7/91

Street Walkers

For five days of unadulterated excitement,
We've walked fifty blocks at a stretch,
Talked nonstop, joked, laughed, waxed cynical,
Shared New York's deepest secrets.
Tonight, we discuss gender discrimination
Women and men demonstrate
In this gossamer Gotham,
Observing how the flesh trade,
As a time-honored profession,
Is left strictly to female exhibitionists
And agents whose bailiwick varies yet pivots
Along Sixth Avenue between 57th
And Central Park South,
Within earshot of Carnegie Hall.

Matisse would have called these ladies of the night
Odalisques, Faulkner courtesans;
I label them "gift whoreses."
Up close, they resemble thirteen-year-old runaways
From Omaha, Wauwatosa, Duluth, and St. Louis,
Daddies' girls gone sadly astray,
Misbegotten nymphs
Rotting from drugs and viruses,
More than devil-may-care temptresses
Dressed in crotch-length, black leather skirts
And see-through, circus-hued blouses,
Reeking of loud perfume,
Modern-day Madonnas
Begging nightly for their baby Jesus.

Strolling back to The Park Lane
From the Symphony Cafe,
I tease my loving, gentle lady,
Pretend to be waving goodbye to her for the weekend
As I slow to let her gain ground,
Then feign an overture to a prostitute
Inching toward me along the curb
Where she works the traffic heading for Columbus Circle.
By quickening her pace,
Janie "encourages" my liaison.
Though I hesitate no more than three seconds,
*

Jane's already crossed the street.
Waiting for the "walk" light, I get distressed
Watching two shadowy beggars converge on her.

Before it changes, I race into the chaos,
Rush to her side, panting,
Just as one of them, a ragged scarecrow,
Shoves a cup into my face, not hers,
Then assaults me with imprecations
When I refuse his rude requests
For money to buy food,
Who may or may not have an annual income
Of $50,000
And doubtless would like to indulge his appetites
For drugs or booze or other men
By using my good intentions to serve his ends.
My fists, clenched in my pockets,
Describe neutered virility.

Once I've outdistanced this tattered pirate,
Who's taunted me with malicious jibes
Because he's arrogated for himself
The right to molest innocents
For the sake of creating an altercation
If he fails to entice his prey
With his speciously heartrending wiles,
It dawns on me that in a space of ten blocks
We've been accosted six times by marauding indigents
And that, indeed, this crippled city
Has been invaded by Visigoths and Huns,
Is being vandalized from within its precincts
And overrun by the have-nots too lazy
To hire on at the sanitation department

Or hawk newspapers and T-shirts;
Worse, their profession is dominated by males
Who, unlike hookers, don't even carry health cards,
Who sleep under cardboard boxes in doorways
And rifle garbage bags for aluminum cans,
Lunch, shoes, used needles.
Yet both sluts and bums are rank-and-file members
Of the oldest union in the world,
*

Soul sellers who trade dignity and spirit
For one more night's survival
And grope from day to day
Living out their ghetto lives
Inside the fences they help society erect
And keep in good repair.

Tonight, as we take the elevator to our room,
Soar forty stories high,
A protective silence envelops Jane and me;
I hear her heartbeat across the empty car,
Intuit her immediate relief,
Knowing she dreads street crime
Yet eagerly desires the exhilaration
That resonates from every subway entrance,
Window, passing taxi, truck, bus,
And interlocking Mondrian plane of pedestrians
Who never seem to collide.
We arrive, exit, head for our lavish room
To relax after walking the streets,
Grateful we don't have to beg for each other's love.

4/8/91

Sun-Struck

This sunny afternoon gladdens my sad heart,
Clears my dispirited ears
So that I can almost hear you calling me
Despite the wide geography
Keeping us from touching each other
With subtle love-notes;
Its soft blue hue
Lets me focus on you
With vision occluded these last few months
For my being lost in a dog-day fog
As I've witnessed my dissolved marriage
Devolve into my children's denial of me.

The sun on my arm and neck,
Shining through the driver's-side window,
Transports my senses:
We're in bed, nakedly enmeshed,
Ecstatic in one undulant communion of flesh,
Two souls breathing the same breath,
Dreaming identical dreams,
Reaching climax simultaneously,
Whose heat is the necessary energy
That illuminates our moon-crazed universe.
Janie, how dark my star would be
Without your rays!

4/24/91

A Trinity of Jewish Poets

We ventured out last night,
An oppressively humid Tuesday,
For a few quality hours of intellect-stretching,
To hear three Jewish poets
Read in their various dialects:
One, from Brooklyn, of Salonikan stock;
A second, born and reared in the Midwest,
Right here in this enclave of Reform Jewry,
St. Louis, Missouri; the third,
A Hebrew-speaking math teacher from Jerusalem —
A respectable trinity.

And what a gamut that trio ran,
From midrashic and cabalistic allegories
To Biblical stories of Abraham, Isaac, Jacob,
Eve, Sarah, and Leah;
Eastern to Sephardic rituals and myths;
Grotesque references ranging from Titus, Hadrian, Pharaoh,
Pétain, Himmler, and Hitler
To every other diabolical archfiend
Who ever threatened the "chosen people"
By committing crimes against humanity;
Family to love to the token, self-reflexive joke.

As we sat, listening intently,
Holding hands as if to reassure each other
We really belonged within this literary setting
And that the issues being articulated
Were relevant to us,
We both began to squeeze tightly, tenderly,
Feel the blood pulsing in our fingers.
Gradually, we heard inner voices singing,
Connecting us to the cadences of the poets,
Transporting us to a heritage we'd neglected
For more than forty years — people of the Word.

5/22/91

Memorial Day

Our thoughts this long weekend
Are just not focused
On commemorating those lost in this nation's wars
But rather on celebrating our defeat
Of the forces of dysfunction and divorce,
Those Axis powers
Dedicated to the destruction
Of entire societies from within,
The ultimate collaboration of invisible Vichy.
We relax, devote these precious hours
To assessing the progress of our victory garden,
Taking note of growth and other changes:

Nicotianas and geraniums in clay pots
Have started to spring up;
A solitary nodule from the leafy tomato plants
Signals the beginning of lusty fruit;
A delicate blue bloom
Is suspended from a vine,
So far the only one
Out of four hanging baskets of plumbago;
A single, stunning fuchsia swings in the air,
Its pendulous pink-and-white Chinese lanterns
Drooping in profuse quietude;
Hibiscus blossoms, giant vermillion butterflies,

Continue to materialize daily,
As if their three man-high trees
Will never stop producing new beauty.
Satisfied that we've fortified love's garden,
We turn to each other for succor.
But as we do so, my lady spies in the tufted grass
A snowy cluster of clovers she picks,
Then, stem after stem, loops,
Slipping another flower through each, and knots,
Until she's completed a chain,
Affection's honorary ribbon,
She places around her hero's neck.

5/28/91

Hibiscus Love

Each morning, as I slip from the house —
Coaxing my car to a local café
For coffee and toast
And a dose of the newspaper's recent events,
Then to my writing office,
Where the Scylla and Charybdis forces of my occupation
Suck my euphoric spirit into their vortex
Before casting it onto afternoon's blanched shore
Like tide-worn coral —
My eyes light on the tightly closed blooms
Of the three hibiscus trees bordering the patio.

Each 5 p.m., when I arrive home,
My soul washed back to the floor of the ocean
That transports me along its workaday currents,
I park, sling the strap of my attaché over my shoulder,
And meander wearily into the garden,
Where, amidst potted petunias, geraniums, nicotianas,
Hanging baskets of fuchsias and plumbagos,
And drumstick alliums lifting above impatiens in planters,
Grow those glorious hibiscus flowers,
Open so wide now
They invite me into their sensuous funnels to hide.

Inside one, I find its scented temple-quietude
Provides sweet refuge for my tired mind;
Hydra-headed anxieties
Still clinging to my spinal cord and brain
Let go their lampreylike holds.
As if filled with helium, my entire being
Rises into a zone of pure innocence.
Slowly my components coalesce,
Metamorphose into a delicate bloom
You just might notice among such lushness
And recognize as your prince in his hibiscus disguise.

6/18/91

Skybiscus

It's one of the clearest nights of the season;
The sky over St. Louis
Whistles with the intricate maneuverings
Of byzantine constellations,
Meteor showers, asteroid belts,
Planets, and moons stippling space
With their precarious interrelatedness.
Janie and I gaze at this decorated curtain
Separating its stage from our growing impatience —
After all, the show *was* to begin
Promptly at nine this Fourth of July.

Having worked the whole holiday,
Disregarding its ukase to rest, relax,
Recover from numbing routine,
We try to salvage at least a semblance of patriotism
By braving the peaceful hordes
Streaming into Kirkwood for twenty minutes of fireworks,
"The **BEST AND BRIGHTEST** in pyrotechnics,"
A jingoistic coterie of small-business owners
Constituting the town's chamber of commerce
Has boasted in neighborhood and citywide newspapers
In hopes of capitalizing on a local event.

We locate a scrap of unoccupied grass,
From whose dubious vantage,
Amidst the gleeful screams
Kids of every age, race, and persuasion
Will soon unleash in uninhibited affirmation
As though each shriek were a balloon
They'll spontaneously let loose
Just to empathize with its fuguelike freedom,
We witness white, middle-class America,
Its two-income families mortgaged to the nines,
Their cyberspace offspring pressing all the wrong buttons.

Abruptly we're assaulted by a salute
Of raucous reports ten seconds apart;
Thousands of strangers go momentarily crazy
Recognizing "Beethoven's" *1812* Overture,
Respond with reverence bordering on zealotry
*

As if high priests were stoking the fires
In preparation for human sacrifice.
Unannounced, Chinese skyrockets,
Assembled in Texas by Mexicans
And installed by Japanese technicians,
Appear as surreptitiously as illegal aliens.

Within minutes, the whole bowl of the universe,
Which earlier disclosed heavenly bodies,
Blurs with smoke from detonating gunpowder,
Turns acrid from spent sulfur and saltpeter;
Were it not for the brilliant flashes
Splashing the welkin with symmetrical girandoles,
We might believe we were under siege
By a hazy, thermal inversion over the city,
Not the noxious, toxic by-products of such beauty.
One by one, these sumptuous flowers blossom:
Spider mums, hibiscuses, plumbagos

Explode in rapid profusion,
Budding, blooming, drooping, dying.
We partake of their evanescent efflorescing,
Postpone whatever cynicism
We might have vented on the drive over,
And submit to the simple magic of the moment,
All of us suburban stargazers,
Allowing ourselves to experience infrequent passion
And escape into a zone of rare emotions.
By degrees, each of us, in his own way,
Reaches epiphany, achieves personal apotheosis.

Too suddenly, an orgy of swirling lights
Spraying up and out in every direction,
Intersecting one another's dazzling trajectories,
Signals the unwished-for finish of this year's celebration.
Thousands of hearts miss a few beats,
Many throats momentarily choke,
And twice that many eyes widen
As the spasm expends itself,
Seeks refuge in dark silence.
We rush off to avoid the massive traffic jam
And say nothing until we find our car.

Sympathetic words fail us,
Seem so inappropriate in this chaotic aftermath.
In moments like this, our cynicism marries us:
Janie and I become Mr. and Mrs. Diogenes.
We fire our own fusillade of wisecracks and snide asides
To celebrate our independence from sentimentality —
We've just seen America at its worst,
The belligerent, insular innocence
Inherent in our national identity,
The spendthrift blend of extravagance and penury
We're reborn to every Fourth of July.

7/5/91

Nightflowers

There's nothing less romantic
Than silk forsythias, tulips, tiger lilies,
And artificial pussy willows
Arranged with studied offhandedness
In vases and clay pots in hotel lobbies,
Like those in Memphis' Peabody,
New Orleans' Monteleone,
And the Adam's Mark in St. Louis,
Where, this cool, mid-July evening,
My lady and I rendezvous a few intimate hours
To listen to Ptah Williams
Stroke notes from his jazz piano
That coalesce as "Maple Leaf Rag,"
"Going to Kansas City,"
"Basin Street Blues," and "Ain't Misbehavin'."

There's nothing that ruins the ambiance as quickly
As fake forsythias and other ersatz creations
Except when they beguile me into believing
That flowers exist perpetually,
Not just for a brief Missouri season,
And depend on nothing but the love we engender
Whenever we spend the evening together
Gazing into each other's soft, sweet, smiling eyes.
It's then that imitations like these
Transport us back to imagination, the heart's oasis,
That garden in which all things grow,
And you and I remember spring is an endless beginning,
A promise we renew whenever we venture out
To plant ourselves, side by side,
In a universe of blossoming possibilities.

7/13/91

Love's Litany

Sunday a.m. is the one moment in the week
When our spirits take leave of their senses,
Cancel all routines,
And seize secular sanctity just by breathing,
Entering time's suspension,
Where ecstasy and silence
Create a voluptuously intricate enchantment
Using the two of us,
Sleeping nude in our Garden of Eden bed,
As protégés upon whose psyches
They might debut their newest music and dreams.

We drowse deeply beneath beguilement's surface,
Conscious of neither philters
Coercing us toward morning's orgasm
Nor reverberations, emanating from Earth's core,
Metamorphosing us into Brancusi seals
Or Henry Moore lovers
Constantly reshaping their stone-woven pose.
Not realizing we've been charmed,
We awaken by degrees into the most blessed synesthesia
Humans, Keats' *amateurs* included, can experience
And, touching, discover each other's innocence.

Face to face in horizontal embrace,
We assimilate sleep's dissipating fragrances,
Savor those saline odors of body heat
And matted hair, wetted and dried
Throughout the night.
You guide your fingertips over my eyelids,
Across my lips, down my stomach, down;
I measure the contours of your breasts,
Ribs, supple belly; descending,
My right hand transcribes your hips and thighs;
I come to rest inside you.

In this sacred temple of our choosing,
Where no rabbi, priest, or itinerant minister
Disseminates virtuous learning —
The recorded Word of the Lord —
By excerpting chapters and verses
*

From gospels and rites of passage in the Pentateuch,
We repeat the litany of our lovemaking,
Whisper its spontaneous phrases in each other's ears
As our spirits achieve resurrection,
And pray that our adoration and trust
Will sustain us until dust appropriates our passion.

7/28/91

Gaining a Better Perspective

Occasionally, my lady and I
Spontaneously decide
To quit whatever we might be doing
And drive down to Laclede's Landing for lunch,
As we did this Sunday,
To watch towboats guiding their barges
Between piers of the Eads Bridge
Like slow-motion shuttles through looms,

Listen to freight trains,
Drawn by red diesel yard-switchers
Of the Terminal Railroad Association,
Clatter over trestles paralleling the Mississippi,
Their hoppers weighted to the breaking point
With coal from Peabody mines
Dotting southern Illinois,
And maybe even glimpse the *Delta Queen.*

On a lark, we'll head downtown,
Park near the Gateway Arch
To picnic or, like yesterday,
Sit outdoors at Sundecker's
To absorb the aura,
Nibble grilled chicken sandwiches and hamburgers,
And reflect on a pocket of the city
Most citizens have relegated to history.

Paradoxically, we take great pleasure
In collecting shards of St. Louis' past
And piecing them together with imagination's glue,
Recreating the original inspiration
That shaped from Chouteau's sloping strand
This complex metropolis,
As though perpetuating our future together
Depends on seeing the present through older eyes.

7/29/91

A Double Wedding

How relaxing
To be missing in action
This Sunday afternoon in Rochester,
We two waifs
Taking a planned detour
On our way from St. Louis to Boston,

Compatible stowaways on a cosmic ship,
Milkweed seeds
Aquiver in the breeze,
Visitors strolling along the Genesee River,
Transmuting its shimmer
Into memories lingering from the wedding
Of a friend's daughter,
Which we attended last evening,

Listening now
To our own unspoken vows commending us —
Lovers to the end.

8/4/91

Our Boston Tea Party

For three days and nights,
Janie and I have explored Boston,
Shared insights and opinions
Schoolchildren on a field trip to Neptune might have.
We've experienced delight
Reconstructing from the few remaining artifacts
The history of dissidence, anarchy,
And the ultimate establishment of democracy,
Whose original ballast still steadies our ship of state.

But, oh, what imagination it takes
To envision people as they were, events as they occurred,
And ideologies as they were meant to reflect.
It's difficult to assess authenticity
When the old Quincy Markets
Have been appropriated by The Sharper Image,
Brookstone, The Nature Company,
Doubleday, The Gap, Banana Republic,
ACA Joe's, Victoria's Secret,

A hundred sundry greasy eateries
Promulgating Buffalo wings and potato skins,
And a thousand pseudo-Irish pubs
Serving a million tons of clam chowder per hour
To modern pilgrims on the run
From one mall to another across the country,
As though homogeneity were not just a plague
But a way of life, a viable alternative
To discovering a shorter route to the next New World.

Even Faneuil Hall cringes in disrepute,
Threatened by eight glittering floors of The Limited,
Its parasitical Siamese twin,
With which it will have to compete after renovation.
What's it going to be?
Saks? Neiman Marcus? Henri Bendel?
Maybe in its newest avatar
It will achieve transcendence as Crabtree & Evelyn!
But can it survive at $5,000 a square foot?

We grope for refuge from sensory persecution,
Trying to assert our inalienable needs
For freedom of speech,
Unfettered political expression,
And liberation from the tyranny of spiritual taxation
Imposed by mediocrity and hypocrisy
And unjustified by the divine right of Presidents,
Who, usurping too much power,
Elude Congressional checks and balances

And form their own elite Ministry of Propaganda,
Replete with Nixonian Gestapo,
To effect accidental fascism
By proxied consent of a drowsing populace.
How decidedly creative
Tourists of today's Boston must be
To extrapolate myth from vestiges of Beacon Hill,
King's Chapel, the Granary, the Old State House,
And the Old North and South Churches,

Especially when it's so tempting to let replicas,
Statues, facsimiles, artists' renderings
Serve for that which has perished through acts of God
Or dubious human "progress."
Ah, but what choice do we really have?
Although we can visit the architect's guess
At the original structure that housed Paul Revere,
Were it not for Longfellow and Grant Wood
There would be little romance, far less drama,

Notwithstanding the fact that the accuracy of fact
Has taken a backseat to truth.
Who cares anyway, Janie and I finally ask ourselves,
Tripping over cobblestones, crossing under the expressway,
Retreating to our overpriced Long Wharf digs?
Perhaps the Founding Fathers had our best interests,
As well as theirs, at heart
When, upon signing the Declaration of Independence,
They licensed dissent in its many guises and intents.

8/7/91

A Part of History

So much history lingers in this city
That I feel like a kid on a scavenger hunt
Whenever I take to its sidewalks or streets.
Just today, returning from Cambridge,
Accidentally exiting the "T" at Government Crossing,
Janie and I found ourselves near Filene's,
Briefly disoriented,
Overshadowed by high finance's obelisks.
By degrees, we reached the Old State House,
Then headed down to the harbor,
Where our hotel marks the start of the Long Wharf.

It's hard to get lost in Boston:
Although only ghosts, both patriots and redcoats
(Adams, Hancock, Revere, Gage, Burgoyne, Howe)
Keep making their nearness felt,
Just as landmarks like Faneuil Hall
And the Old North Church
Continue to remind us of their perpetuity.
This very minute, sitting on a bench at wharf's end,
Kissing each other in extended embrace,
My love and I, like the British did,
Enter this city's history for a few fiery heartbeats.

8/7/91

Picking Love Apples

So much turbulence has scourged my life
These past three years,
So agonizingly slow and thorough in their unfolding,
That I've grown used to seizing
The seemingly least dramatic event
And heightening any trivial ritual
With hyperbolic significance,
Redefining the contours of its reality
By making it conform to cadences
Instead of shapes with dimension and weight.
Take, for instance, Janie's tomato plants —

Oh, wait just a minute, gentle reader;
Indulge me, if you'll be so kind,
A brief digression from the present issue
To state the nature of my purpose
This tranquil Sunday morning,
First by proclaiming my thanks to the Fates
For having relocated me, a divorcé,
In a stable relationship in which the lady of the house
Is accepting of the fact that my poet's credentials
Are useless in the eyes of a fast-food society
Consumed by its own conspicuous consumption,

Then by simply explaining why,
After nearly three decades,
My spirit-guided psyche,
Obsessed with the music of the spheres,
Still craves hearing in its vague emanations
Strains so fluidly soothing to the ears
My juices begin pulsing like moon-tuned tides
And bones and flesh faintly reverberate
Until my entire physical being
Reconnects with my senses and intellect
In an act of devout, if secular, communion with existence . . .

Whoa! Where am I? How have I allowed myself
To stray so academically,
So didactically, from this spacious living room,
Where, with coffee beside me, ledger on my lap,
And magic wand in hand,
*

I'm now staring through the plate-glass window,
Past nicotianas in clay pots
And hibiscus trees bordering the patio,
To the small garden laced with lettuce, dill,
Parsley, Gerber daisies,
And, most impressive, six tomato plants,

All of them taller than Janie herself,
Who, as I sit here contemplating
Why I've let the creative process lapse,
Compels me to abandon pen and paper,
Run outdoors, throw off my bathrobe,
And wrap my arms around her from behind
In a spontaneous gesture of passion?
As if to emulate her judicious choosing of fruit,
I gently squeeze her breasts
And suggest we conclude this harvest
In our garden's other bed.

8/18/91

Apotheosis on a Sunday Morning

I awaken sedately this mid-September morning
And enter the temple of solitude
Not to pray but to commune with the nature of the universe
Molecule by molecule, atom for atom —
A presumptuous undertaking, if I say so myself!
With coffee, ledger book, and pen,
The tools of my trade, I venture past the kitchen
Into the sanctuary of the living room,
Where, steeped in stunning silence,
I seek a vantage from which looking and listening
Will connect me with the ritual of existence.

Massive plate-glass windows,
Facing the backyard and side patio,
Provide the exits for imagination to escape,
Engage the colors, sounds, and shapes
That, interfacing, form the design of the beyond,
And bring me in touch with what I believe
May be the essence of God's divinity,
That *joie de vivre* infusing everything I say and write,
From my most trivial "hello"
To my most majestic closure of each *Prelude*,
Leaves of Grass, and *Paradise Lost* I create from scratch.

As I gaze out, vision encounters a series of scenes:
Green bowers of two colossal oaks
Improvising a stately ballet on the breeze's stage;
Birds converging on these three acres
To forage for worms forced to the surface
By automatic sprinklers — cardinals, starlings,
Sparrows, robins, pileated woodpeckers,
And predatory blue jays screeching imperiously;
Four-inch-wide, five-petaled hibiscus blooms
Flaunting their luminous orange-red hues
As if taunting the sun to confess it's met its match.

Suddenly, the lady whom I left sleeping
When I slipped from bed, from our dark room,
To fix morning's brew and ready my poetic head
For a spell of metaphoric searches and seizures
Appears among the tomato plants;
*

Wending in and out of nicotianas, liriopes, and buddleias,
She speaks to me in a graceful terpsichore,
Whose gentle symmetry is so beautiful to my senses
My eyes can't keep my ears from hearing them cry
Or my heart from recognizing this excess
As the apotheosis of my happiness.

9/15/91

Too Many Irons

From Wednesday evening to Sunday afternoon,
My lady and I, in a whirlwind flourish,
Have experienced such a cultural salmagundi
That even P. T. Barnum might find himself speechless
Assessing the ingenuity it's taken
Just to maintain our equanimity
Under the marathon gamut of entertainment
Ranging from a three-hour staging of *Cyrano de Bergerac*,
To the St. Louis Symphony
Playing William Schuman, Edward Elgar,
And Antonín Dvořák's lyrical *New World* composition,

To the last matinée of a week-long engagement
Of "The Greatest Show on Earth,"
Encamped at The Arena. Oh, what a potpourri
Janie and I have tasted these past five days!
What absolute alchemy
To have one's life changed by an oversized nose,
Oboe and B-flat clarinet solos,
And a center-ring cage containing two lions,
A trio of tigers, a quartet of leopards,
And a pair of black bears performing on cue
To the whip-crack of an Italian trainer.

Oh, how our psyches reel this Monday morning!
Even mainlining strong coffee
Doesn't seem to wake us,
Lift our spirits from an abyss of depression
Over the cessation of all that imagistic stimulation,
Or clear the dizziness unsettling our concentration,
Keeping our goals for the week ahead from coalescing,
Letting us get a focus on them.
Curious how we can't forget dying Cyrano
Proclaiming his undying love
For the mistress of his unrequited devotion, Roxanne;

Can't expunge from our humming ears
Those compelling themes of the largo movement
And the other no less sensuous motifs
The Bohemian reiterated with striking precision
As he rose from his American ashes and returned to Prague;
*

Can't dismiss from memory's Ringling Bros. Circus
Fairies dangling by their hair fifty feet in the air,
Scantily clad riders mounted atop elephants,
Fifteen in all, as gentle as they are colossal,
A rhinoceros circling inside a cage at *his* pace,
And those zany clowns perforating tension-laced acts

To allow crews time to raise safety nets
For trapezists, tightrope walkers, aerial motorcyclists
And sweep away the obligatory urine and dung
No felines, canines, ursi, equines,
Simians, and pachyderms (humans too)
Could possibly be expected to resist purging
Despite rigidly kept feeding schedules.
Sitting here with this severe case of sensory overload,
We seriously consider going back to bed
And postponing indefinitely — until Tuesday —
Cramming our calendar for the week ahead.

9/16/91

The Two Trees

Janie . . . just invoking your name,
As Milton did his muse
At the stirring, blank-verse opening of *Paradise Lost*,
In hope of triggering a poem,
Makes me shiver with the excitement of imminent discovery.
The whole life-force haloing my soul,
Protecting memory from forgetting's nematodes,
Illuminating the maze leading subterraqueously
From Calvary's tomb to the gates of heaven,
Lies before me, like the Lord's glorious kingdom,
Which Satan showed Christ, whenever I say your name.

Janie . . . Janie! Oh, how the shape of that sound,
As though it were a magician's wand,
Parts history's Red Sea,
Letting me pass between all gone civilizations
Back to the beginning, to that mythic garden
Where, so we've been told by every poet
And voice of Scriptural authority,
The first two humans confronted their mortality,
Comprehended the immense consequences
Their loss of innocence would have for future generations,
And, accepting their limited destiny, began their adventure.

Gazing through the plate-glass windows
Separating me from radiant October,
I see us, Janie,
Hand in hand, just us two,
Standing beneath a pair of huge oak trees
Recently shorn of diseased limbs,
Rendered empty, barren,
Vulnerable for their exposed crosscuts;
Just us two, so new to each other,
Preparing to set off with wandering steps and slow,
Robed only in trust, married in a shared covenant of love.

10/5/91

The Golden Apples of the Sun

After "The Song of Wandering Aengus,"
by William Butler Yeats

This crystalline midweek morning,
I leave the city behind,
Abandon dreams long gone to seed,
Which I had no need for in the first place,
Though, at that age,
No amount of clairvoyance
Could have made me change my fate
Or persuaded me to deviate
From taking those paths of least resistance
I feverishly believed
Would lead me to the Land of the Sacred Tree,
Beyond the westernmost extremities
Of the Islands of the Blessed, the Hesperides,
Where I would appropriate Gaea's golden apples
From their rightful owner
And return from my extended voyage
Hoping to bestow them on my own youthful wife.

Today, a divorcé, separated from my children,
Exiled to the Isle of Diaspora,
Yet free to wander like Aengus and Oisin
Or Moses through myriad wildernesses
Within the Desert of Loneliness,
I drive deep into the hinterland seeking a dream
That only recently has redeemed my spirit
From despondency so severe
Memory had forgotten its name,
Breathing the heart's raison d'être.
On a whim, I've ventured out
In search of my new muse, Lady Jane,
Who, I know, is waiting to succor me,
Help me stay young by reciprocating my sublimated love,
And allow me to entrust to her safekeeping
Those apples I appropriated —
Apples to be savored in our golden years together.

10/9/91

Making Sweet Music

Janie and I escape into Friday evening
Seeking our weekly fix
Of music filtering through the Ritz's lobby;
We can't resist its opiates.
Frequently, we make this trip after dining late
Or visiting with acquaintances
To listen for a few unintruded hours
To the accomplished duo,
Pianist and double bassist,
Who perform such smooth standards
We lose ourselves to their gently blended cadences,
Ascend their stairway to the entrance
Beyond which sensuous enchantments reverberate,
And, squeezing each other's hands,
Disappear into their beguilement.

Oh, what a way to go slowly nowhere
Just below pleasure's threshold.
For an indeterminate eon or so,
We leave behind all human identity,
Become piano and contrabass,
Succumb to their strings' obbligatos to love.
Soon, the sounds will come unwound,
And the musicians will dissolve into the fugitive night;
Later, lying in naked embrace,
We'll both be humming romantic ballads
They never even played.

10/25/91

In Praise of Thanksgivings

Haloed by the pungent fragrance of paper-whites
Radiating into this spacious living room,
Competing with silence for preeminence,
My senses awaken to the celebration of themselves:
A secular ecstasy is in progress
This Thanksgiving morning;
I can almost hear my spirit being borne back
To that desolate Atlantic shoreline
Where the Pilgrims landed 370 years ago
To appropriate from the New World wilderness
Just enough elbowroom and breathing space
To practice peaceful beliefs,
Promulgate God-fearing ways,
And propagate their fledgling confederacy
With immunity from self-appointed prelates
Imbued with the divine right of kings.

I, like those exiles, have, of necessity,
Been obliged to leave behind family and friends
To gain this precarious purchase
And reassert my stifled need for freedom
To worship whatever essence of monotheism
I might choose and, in choosing,
Lose myself to all possibilities of human volition.
I too have immigrated
To the heart's sparsely inhabited land
To proclaim that who I am and what I do
Are virtues exempt from review;
They render me an independent agent
Capable of accomplishing mystical deeds
Just by heeding the call to appreciate small things,
Like the smell of blooming paper-whites
And the way you welcome me home at the end of the day.

11/28/91

Old-Fashioned Family Dinner at Home

Janie, her two sons, and I
Dine together tonight;
We range in age from fifteen to fifty,
With sensibilities running the gamut
From World War II to Desert Storm,
A far more formidable sign of disparity
Than mere comparison of our years might suggest.
The boys chastise us for resorting to anachronisms
And abstruse references to the past:
"Cakes" for bars of soap,
Fireside chats, *Fibber McGee and Molly*,
"By jingo by gee by gosh by gum."
She asks Michael what it means to him
That her grandparents used to sit nightly "watching" the radio.

He has no clue that his passive participation
With the ubiquitous "box"
Has neutered not only *his* imagination
But that of the last generation and a half,
Rendered them incapable of dreaming,
Seeing past fact to truth
Independent of "leading economic indicators,"
Booze ads, rappers, martial artists,
Movie stars and Magic-al athletes with HIV,
Turbocharged cars with spoilers,
Mix-and-match sex, porn flicks,
And presidential, "read my lips" vetoes.
Mike's silence provokes us,
Yet we hesitate getting didactic with him.

Jane and I have probably seen too much
During the three-plus decades
We have on him,
Suffered way too much disillusion
Over acts of gratuitous cruelty,
Political and evangelical hypocrisy,
Wall Street junk-bond greed,
And, right in our own suburban backyard,
Sewer pipes freezing,
Bursting from not being set deep enough,
Shingles peeling, gutters rusting, roofs leaking
*

For construction companies rigging bids
With subcontractors who augment their kickbacks
By installing inferior materials.

Yes, we refrain,
Realizing this teenager may be better off than we
For growing up without hope of an improved future,
A computer wizard used to viewing screens for hours,
Inputting his cynicism on floppy disks,
Witnessing televised murder and verbal abuse,
Experiencing divorce-wars firsthand,
And having adolescent drug lords imitating Noriega
In his own school corridors.
And where has all our imagination taken us anyway?
Here we sit, the four of us,
Discussing cakes of soap, *Fibber McGee*,
Those golden days of radio,
And why Janie and I never seem to watch TV.

12/6/91

Love-Blooms

Sitting here in this quiet living room,
Imbibing permeating fragrances
Sweet Sunday morning
Appropriates from its blooming congregation
Of amaryllises, paper-whites, and stars-of-Bethlehem,
I awaken to an imminent revelation
Half haloing vision's horizon
Like a rainbow rising,
Widening miles behind a summer thunderstorm.

Suddenly I recognize you, Janie,
Gently, sensually efflorescing,
Your naked petals slowly opening before me,
Forming an oval, a tunnel, a funnel
Down which I tumble,
Like a bumblebee seeking the golden stores
At the core of hibiscus and lilac,
Until I'm in your orb,
As I was last night, absorbed in your love.

12/8/91

A Month of Sundays, or Three

Most Sunday mornings,
It seems as though the locus of my soul,
Its corporeal seat, anyway,
The sensory essence of my being's intellect,
Settles into the silent,
Paper-white-scented dimensions
Of your open living room
To recollect in moments of tranquillity
The week's modest and monumental events,
Unspoken kindnesses we showed each other,
Dialogues we wove, riddles we unraveled,
Then select from that trove of homespun treasures
Just one golden thread
With which to sew a poetic Joseph-robe,
A token of devotion
To protect you with my love all week.

12/15/91

Christmas Flowers

With just ten days left till Christmas,
You'd think we'd be decking the house
With pink and red poinsettias
Instead of making such a fuss
Over tall stalks of paper-white clusters
Freshly blooming in their crystal bowls
And the solitary, eighteen-inch-high,
Three-blossom amaryllis rising from its stem,
Whose bulb you forced a month ago,
When November seemed so far away
From this Sunday morning
On which you and I now admire them tenderly,
Like friends we've known,
Though haven't spoken with, since childhood.

We congregate in the living room,
Flowers and humans sensitive to each other's space,
Incarnations of goddesses and gods
Coexisting under the same roof
In a peace-loving covenant of grace,
Monotheistic in our mutual celebration of Christmas,
Toward which, tropistically, we incline.
Sitting on this soft sofa,
Witnessing these plants growing
Infinitesimally,
We imagine how they perceive our presence here,
See ourselves from their point of view —
Two blooms populating an entire universe
With the fragrance of naked newborns.

12/15/91

Christmas Reflections

Janie, you may not believe a word
Of what I'm about to tell you,
But it's the gospel.
Whether an optical illusion, prismatic trick,
Or numinous transmutation of the truth,
The revelation I had this Christmas morning
Occurred just this way:
I stirred early to a silent house,
Decided to let you sleep,
Keep sugarplum dreams dancing in your head,
While I seized the interlude to commune with myself,
Perhaps compose a love poem for you
On this sacred occasion
Of the Christ child's birth.

But as I entered the living room,
Inhaling the penetrating scent
Lifting from a bowl of newly bloomed paper-whites,
My eyes were struck by a majestic sight
Flaming like meteorites
Through the translucent sheers
Veiling both plate-glass windows —
Millions of microcosmic dots
That, when I drew back the diaphanous drapes,
Disclosed not yards stippled with frost
Refracting iridescently from the rising sun
But King Solomon's treasure,
Its faceted gems
Casting miraculous, glowing coronas:

Rubies, emeralds, sapphires, diamonds,
Onyxes, opals, regal amethysts,
And tiger's-eyes
Glinting off the dormant grass
As if their shafts might blind me
With such magnificence.
I stared as long as my senses dared
Before turning away, resetting my focus
On objects less likely to dizzy my imagination,
Crazy me to seek metaphysical explanations
*

For this perfectly natural phenomenon.
But the persistence of vision,
Having etched my retinas with those rays,
Has had the strangest effect on me all day:

I haven't been able to take my gaze off of you.
Your slender arms and narrow wrists,
Ending in tiny hands and delicate fingers,
Are those of a Jumeau doll;
Your radiant blond hair
Halos your face like Cimabue's Madonna;
Your eyes sparkle as if fissures deep inside them
Were absorbing the earth's darkness
And emanating divine light;
Your glistening lips
Invite me to celebrate with you, this Christmas,
The communion of our loving spirits.
It seems every time we kiss,
You're born unto me again.

12/25/91

Biographical Note

Louis Daniel Brodsky was born in St. Louis, Missouri, in 1941, where he attended St. Louis Country Day School. After earning a B.A., magna cum laude, at Yale University in 1963, he received an M.A. in English from Washington University in 1967 and an M.A. in Creative Writing from San Francisco State University the following year.

Mr. Brodsky is the author of thirty-three volumes of poetry, five of which have been published in French by Éditions Gallimard. His poems have appeared in *Harper's*, *Southern Review*, *Texas Quarterly*, *National Forum*, *Ariel*, *American Scholar*, *Kansas Quarterly*, Ball State University's *Forum*, *New Welsh Review*, *Cimarron Review*, *Orbis*, and *Literary Review*, as well as in five editions of the *Anthology of Magazine Verse and Yearbook of American Poetry*.

Also available from **Time Being Books**

LOUIS DANIEL BRODSKY
You Can't Go Back, Exactly
The Thorough Earth
Four and Twenty Blackbirds Soaring
Mississippi Vistas: Volume One of *A Mississippi Trilogy*
Falling from Heaven: Holocaust Poems of a Jew and a Gentile
  (with William Heyen)
Forever, for Now: Poems for a Later Love
Mistress Mississippi: Volume Three of *A Mississippi Trilogy*
A Gleam in the Eye: Poems for a First Baby
Gestapo Crows: Holocaust Poems
The Capital Café: Poems of Redneck, U.S.A.
Disappearing in Mississippi Latitudes: Volume Two of *A
  Mississippi Trilogy*

HARRY JAMES CARGAS (editor)
Telling the Tale: A Tribute to Elie Wiesel on the Occasion of His
  65th Birthday — Essays, Reflections, and Poems

JUDITH CHALMER
Out of History's Junk Jar: Poems of a Mixed Inheritance

GERALD EARLY
How the War in the Streets Is Won: Poems on the Quest of Love
  and Faith

ROBERT HAMBLIN
From the Ground Up: Poems of One Southerner's Passage to
  Adulthood

WILLIAM HEYEN
Erika: Poems of the Holocaust:
Falling from Heaven: Holocaust Poems of a Jew and a Gentile
  (with Louis Daniel Brodsky)
Pterodactyl Rose: Poems of Ecology
Ribbons: The Gulf War — A Poem
The Host: Selected Poems, 1965–1990

TED HIRSCHFIELD
German Requiem: Poems of the War and the Atonement of a
Third Reich Child

VIRGINIA V. JAMES HLAVSA
Waking October Leaves: Reanimations of a Small-Town Girl

RODGER KAMENETZ
The Missing Jew: New and Selected Poems

NORBERT KRAPF
Somewhere in Southern Indiana: Poems of Midwestern Origins

ADRIAN LOUIS
Blood Thirsty Savages

JOSEPH MEREDITH
Hunter's Moon: Poems from Boyhood to Manhood

BEN MILDER
The Good Book Says . . . : Light Verse to Illuminate the Old
Testament

TIME BEING BOOKS
POETRY IN SIGHT AND SOUND
St. Louis, Missouri

FOR OUR FREE CATALOG OR TO ORDER
(800) 331-6605 Monday through Friday
FAX: (314) 432-7939